THE SHROUD OF TURIN

Mystery Revealed

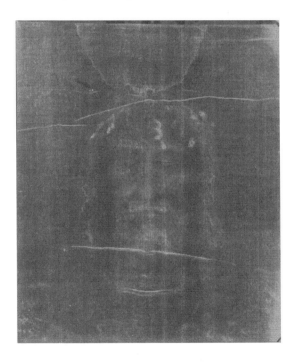

MATT DOLLAR

Copyright 2014. Matt Dollar. All rights reserved.

This Book is not to be sold. It is to be obtained by making a gift donation of only $10 or more.

This book is dedicated to the memory of my grandfather Rev. E.M. Dollar.

The gift donation is to cover printing and publication. Not information contained within.

This publication is subject to all copyright laws, and may not be reproduced or copied in any way without prior written permission from the author(s) of the contained information. Some information in this printed matter is considered public domain and is used as such.

The information contained in this book is all based on scientific facts, previous studies by known shroud and forensic researchers and on the written gospels of Jesus Christ.

Any worthy credit, studies or pictures will receive credit as it appears in this publication.

Early artistic drawing above shows shroud of Turin.

Matt Dollar – Turin historian and book author.

The Shroud of Turin or Turin Shroud is a length of linen cloth bearing the image of a man who appears to have suffered physical trauma in a manner consistent with crucifixion. There is no consensus yet on exactly how the image was created, and it is believed by some to be the burial shroud of Jesus of Nazareth, despite radiocarbon dating placing its origins in the Medieval period.[1] The image is much clearer in black-and-white negative than in its natural sepia color. The negative image was first observed in 1898, on the reverse photographic plate of amateur photographer Secondo Pia, who was allowed to photograph it while it was being exhibited in the Turin Cathedral. The shroud is kept in the royal chapel of the Cathedral of Saint John the Baptist in Turin, northern Italy.

The origins of the shroud and its image are the subject of intense debate among theologians, historians and researchers. Scientific and popular publications have presented diverse arguments for both authenticity and possible methods of forgery. A variety of scientific theories regarding the shroud have since been proposed, based on disciplines ranging from chemistry to biology and medical forensics to optical image analysis. The Catholic Church has neither formally endorsed nor rejected the shroud, but in 1958 Pope Pius XII approved of the image in association with the devotion to the Holy Face of Jesus. More recently, Pope Francis and his predecessor Pope Benedict XVI have both described the Shroud of Turin as "an icon".

In 1978, a detailed examination carried out by a team of American scientists, called the Shroud of Turin Research Project (STURP), found no reliable evidence of how the image was produced. In 1988 a radiocarbon dating test was performed on small samples of the shroud. The laboratories at the University of Oxford, the University of Arizona, and the Swiss Federal Institute of Technology concurred that the samples they tested dated from the Middle Ages, between 1260 and 1390. The validity and the interpretation of the 1988 tests are still contested by some statisticians, chemists and historians. According to professor Christopher Ramsey of the Oxford Radiocarbon Accelerator Unit in 2011, "There are various hypotheses as to why the dates might not be correct, but none of them stack up." This theory will be gone into greater detail further into this book.

According to former Nature editor Philip Ball, "it's fair to say that, despite the seemingly definitive tests in 1988, the status of the Shroud of Turin is murkier than ever. Not least, the nature of the image and how it was fixed on the cloth remain deeply puzzling". The shroud continues to remain one of the most studied and controversial objects in human history.

Here is a detailed description of the cloth.

The shroud is rectangular, measuring approximately 4.4 × 1.1 m (14.3 × 3.7 ft). The cloth is woven in a three-to-one herringbone twill composed of flax fibrils. Its most distinctive characteristic is the faint, brownish image of a front and back view of a naked man with his hands folded across his groin. The two views are aligned along the midplane of the body and point in opposite directions. The front and back views of the head nearly meet at the middle of the cloth.

Reddish brown stains that have been said to include whole blood are found on the cloth, showing various wounds that, according to proponents, correlate with the yellowish image, the pathophysiology of crucifixion, and the Biblical description of the death of Jesus: However forensic tests conducted on the shroud in the late 70s describe the apparent bloodstains as tempera paint tinted red with hematite, and deny the presence of blood.

Markings on the cloth have been interpreted as follows:

one wrist bears a large, round wound, apparently from piercing (the second wrist is hidden by the folding of the hands)

upward gouge in the side penetrating into the thoracic cavity. Proponents say this was a post-mortem event and there are separate components of red blood cells and serum draining from the lesion

small punctures around the forehead and scalp

scores of linear wounds on the torso and legs. Proponents aver that the wounds are consistent with the distinctive dumbbell wounds of a Roman flagrum.

swelling of the face from severe beatings

streams of blood down both arms. Proponents state that the blood drippings from the main flow occurred in response to gravity at an angle that would occur during crucifixion.

large puncture wounds in the feet as if pierced by a single spike

The details of the image on the shroud are not easily distinguishable by the naked eye, and were first observed after the advent of photography. In May 1898 amateur Italian photographer Secondo Pia was allowed to photograph the shroud and he took the first photograph of the shroud on the evening of May 28, 1898. Pia was startled by the visible image of the negative plate in his darkroom. Negatives of the image give the appearance of a positive image, which implies that the shroud image is itself effectively a negative of some kind. Pia was at first accused of doctoring his photographs, but was vindicated in 1931 when a professional photographer, Giuseppe Enrie, also photographed the shroud and his findings supported Pia's. In 1978 Miller and Pellicori took ultraviolet photographs of the shroud.

The image of the "Man of the Shroud" has a beard, moustache, and shoulder-length hair parted in the middle. He is muscular and tall (various experts have measured him as from 1.70 m, or roughly 5 ft 7 in, to 1.88 m, or 6 ft 2 in).[17] The shroud was damaged in a fire in 1532 in the chapel in Chambery, France. There are some burn holes and scorched areas down both sides of the linen, caused by contact with molten silver during the fire that burned through it in places while it was folded.[18] Fourteen large triangular patches and eight smaller ones were sewn onto the cloth by Poor Clare nuns to repair the damage

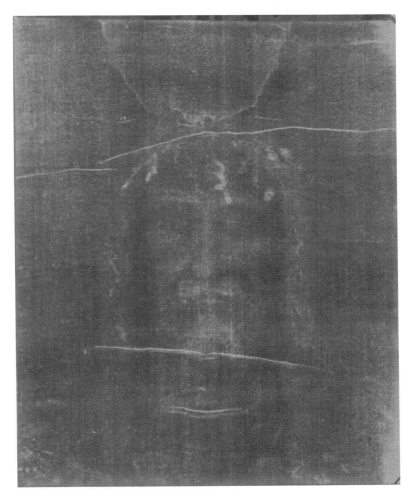

History

The historical records for the shroud can be separated into two time periods: before 1390 and from 1390 to the present. The period until 1390 is subject to debate among historians. Author Ian Wilson has proposed that the Shroud was the Image of Edessa, but scholars such as Averil Cameron have stated that the history of the Image of Edessa represents "very murky territory"; it cannot be traced back as a miraculous image, and it may not have even been a cloth.

Prior to the 14th century there are some congruent references such as the Pray Codex. It is often mentioned that the first certain historical record dates from 1353 or 1357. However the presence of the Turin Shroud in Lirey, France, is only undoubtedly attested in 1390 when Bishop Pierre d'Arcis wrote a memorandum to Antipope Clement VII, stating that the shroud was a forgery and that the artist had confessed. The history from the 15th century to the present is well understood. In 1453 Margaret de Charny deeded the Shroud to the House of Savoy. In 1578 the shroud was transferred in Turin. As of the 17th century the shroud has been displayed (e.g. in the chapel built for that purpose by Guarino Guarini and in the 19th century it was first photographed during a public exhibition.

There are no definite historical records concerning the shroud prior to the 14th century. Although there are numerous reports of Jesus' burial shroud, or an image of his head, of unknown origin, being venerated in various locations before the 14th century, there is no historical evidence that these refer to the shroud currently at Turin Cathedral. A burial cloth, which some historians maintain was the Shroud, was owned by the Byzantine emperors but disappeared during the Sack of Constantinople in 1204.

Historical records seem to indicate that a shroud bearing an image of a crucified man existed in the small town of Lirey around the years 1353 to 1357 in the possession of a French Knight, Geoffroi de Charny, who died at the Battle of Poitiers in 1356. However the correspondence of this shroud with the shroud in Turin, and its very origin has been debated by scholars and lay authors, with statements of forgery attributed to artists born a century apart. Some contend that the Lirey shroud was the work of a confessed forger and murderer.

The history of the shroud from the 15th century is well recorded. In 1532, the shroud suffered damage from a fire in a chapel of Chambéry, capital of the Savoy region, where it was stored. A drop of molten silver from the reliquary produced a symmetrically placed mark through the layers of the folded cloth. Poor Clare Nuns attempted to repair this damage with patches. In 1578 Emmanuel Philibert, Duke of Savoy ordered the cloth to be brought from Chambéry to Turin and it has remained at Turin ever since.

Repairs were made to the shroud in 1694 by Sebastian Valfrè to improve the repairs of the

Poor Clare nuns. Further repairs were made in 1868 by Clotilde of Savoy. The shroud remained the property of the House of Savoy until 1983, when it was given to the Holy.

A fire, possibly caused by arson, threatened the shroud on 11 April 1997. In 2002, the Holy See had the shroud restored. The cloth backing and thirty patches were removed, making it possible to photograph and scan the reverse side of the cloth, which had been hidden from view. A faint part-image of the body was found on the back of the shroud in 2004.

The Shroud was placed back on public display (the 18th time in its history) in Turin from 10 April to 23 May 2010; and according to Church officials, more than 2 million visitors came to see it. Images of the shroud were broadcast on television on 30 March 2013

Religious perspective

Religious beliefs about the burial cloths of Jesus have existed for centuries. The Gospels of

Matthew[27:59-60], Mark[15:46] and Luke[23:53] state that Joseph of Arimathea wrapped the body of Jesus in a piece of linen cloth and placed it in a new tomb. The Gospel of John[19:38-40] refers to strips of linen used by Joseph of Arimathea and states that Apostle Peter found multiple pieces of burial cloth after the tomb was found open, strips of linen cloth for the body and a separate cloth for the head.[20:6-7]

Although pieces of burial cloths of Jesus are held by at least four churches in France and three in Italy, none has gathered as much religious following as the Shroud of Turin. The religious beliefs and practices associated with the shroud predate historical and scientific discussions and have continued in the 21st century, although the Catholic Church has never passed judgment on its authenticity. An example is the Holy Face Medal bearing the image from the shroud, worn by some Catholics.

Criticism by John Calvin

In 1543 John Calvin, in his Treatise on Relics, wrote of the shroud, which was then at Nice (it was moved to Turin in 1578), "How is it possible that those sacred historians, who carefully related all the miracles that took place at Christ's death, should have omitted to mention one so remarkable as the likeness of the body of our Lord remaining on its wrapping sheet?" In an interpretation of the Gospel of John[20:6-7] Calvin concluded that strips of linen were used to cover the body (excluding the head) and a separate cloth to cover the head.[38] He then stated that "either St. John is a liar," or else anyone who promotes such a shroud is "convicted of falsehood and deceit"

Devotions

Although the shroud image is currently associated with Catholic devotions to the Holy Face of Jesus, the devotions themselves predate Secondo Pia's 1898 photograph. Such devotions had been started in 1844 by the Carmelite nun Marie of St Peter (based on "pre-crucifixion" images associated with the Veil of Veronica) and promoted by Leo Dupont, also called the Apostle of the Holy Face. In 1851 Leo Dupont formed the "Archconfraternity of the Holy Face" in Tours, France, well before Secondo Pia took the photograph of the shroud.

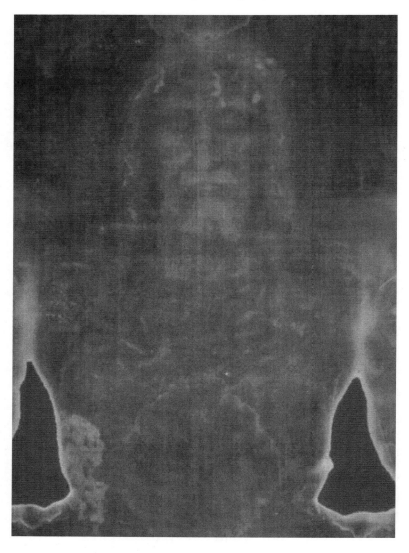

Miraculous image

The religious concept of the "miraculously created image" or acheiropoieton has a long history in Christianity, going back to at least the 6th century. Among the most prominent portable early acheiropoieta are the Image of Camuliana and the Mandylion or Image of Edessa, both painted icons of Christ held in the Byzantine Empire and now generally regarded as lost or destroyed, as is the Hodegetria image of the Virgin. Other early images in Italy, all heavily and unfortunately restored, that have been revered as acheiropoieta now have relatively little following, as attention has focused on the Shroud.

Without debating scientific issues, some believers state as a matter of faith that empirical analysis and scientific methods will perhaps never advance to a level sufficient for understanding the divine methods used for image formation on the shroud, since the body around whom the shroud was wrapped was not merely human, but divine, and believe that the image on the shroud was miraculously produced at the moment of Resurrection.

While most miraculous theories do not attempt to provide explanations, John Jackson (a member of STURP) has proposed that the image was formed by radiation methods beyond the understanding of current science, in particular via the "collapsing cloth" onto a body that was radiating energy at the moment of resurrection. However, STURP member Alan Adler has stated that Jackson's theory is not generally accepted as scientific, given that it runs counter to the known laws of physics.

In 1989 physicist Thomas Phillips, speculated that the Shroud image was formed by neutron radiation due to a miraculous bodily resurrection.

This also happens to be my own personal belief of how the image of Jesus Christ was formed and what I feel was burned into the cloth.

I also believe that God did this so we would have image of the Christ in front of us.

Like the old saying goes "a picture is worth a thousand words".

Vatican position

Antipope Clement VII refrained from expressing his opinion on the shroud; however, subsequent popes from Julius II on took its authenticity for granted.

The Vatican newspaper Osservatore Romano covered the story of Secondo Pia's photograph of May 28, 1898 in its June 15, 1898 edition, but it did so with no comment and thereafter Church officials generally refrained from officially commenting on the photograph for almost half a century.

The first official association between the image on the Shroud and the Catholic Church was made in 1940 based on the formal request by Sister Maria Pierina De Micheli to the curia in Milan to obtain authorization to produce a medal with the image. The authorization was granted and the first medal with the image was offered to Pope Pius XII who approved the medal. The image was then used on what became known as the Holy Face Medal worn by many

Catholics, initially as a means of protection during World War II. In 1958 Pope Pius XII approved of the image in association with the devotion to the Holy Face of Jesus, and declared its feast to be celebrated every year the day before Ash Wednesday. Following the approval by Pope Pius XII, Catholic devotions to the Holy Face of Jesus have been almost exclusively associated with the image on the shroud.

In 1983 the Shroud was given to the Holy See by the House of Savoy. However, as with all relics of this kind, the Roman Catholic Church made no pronouncements on its authenticity. As with other approved Catholic devotions, the matter has been left to the personal decision of the faithful, as long as the Church does not issue a future notification to the contrary. In the Church's view, whether the cloth is authentic or not has no bearing whatsoever on the validity of what Jesus taught nor on the saving power of his death and resurrection.

Pope John Paul II stated in 1998 that: "Since it is not a matter of faith, the Church has no specific competence to pronounce on these questions. She entrusts to scientists the task of continuing to investigate, so that satisfactory answers may be found to the questions connected with this Sheet". Pope John Paul II showed himself to be deeply moved by the image of the Shroud and arranged for public showings in 1998 and 2000. In his address at the Turin Cathedral on Sunday May 24, 1998 (the occasion of the 100th year of Secondo Pia's May 28, 1898 photograph), he said:[52] "The Shroud is an image of God's love as well as of human sin [...] The imprint left by the tortured body of the Crucified One, which attests to the tremendous human capacity for causing pain and death to one's fellow man, stands as an icon of the suffering of the innocent in every age."

In 2000, Cardinal Ratzinger, later to be known as Pope Benedict XVI, wrote that the Shroud of Turin is "a truly mysterious image, which no human artistry was capable of producing. In some inexplicable way, it appeared imprinted upon cloth and believed to show the true face of Christ, the crucified and risen Lord. In June 2008, three years after he assumed the papacy, Pope Benedict announced that the

Shroud would be publicly displayed in the spring of 2010, and stated that he would like to go to Turin to see it along with other pilgrims. During his visit in Turin on Sunday May 2, 2010, Benedict described the Shroud of Turin as an "extraordinary Icon", the "Icon of Holy Saturday corresponding in every way to what the Gospels tell us of Jesus", "an Icon written in blood, the blood of a man who was scourged, crowned with thorns, crucified and whose right side was pierced". The pope said also that in the Turin Shroud "we see, as in a mirror, our suffering in the suffering of Christ". On May 30, 2010, Benedict XVI beatified Sister Maria Pierina De Micheli who coined the Holy Face Medal, based on Secondo Pia's photograph of the Shroud.

On 30 March 2013, as part of the Easter celebrations, there was an extraordinary exposition of the shroud in the Cathedral of Turin. Pope Francis recorded a video message for the occasion, in which he described the image on the shroud as "this Icon of a man", and stated that "the Man of the Shroud invites us to contemplate Jesus of Nazareth." In his carefully worded statement Pope Francis urged the faithful to contemplate the shroud with awe, but "stopped firmly short of asserting its authenticity.

Early Christian writings

A manuscript called the Gospel of the Hebrews (2nd Century) which is not extant other than a dozen lines quoted by Origen, Jerome and Eusebius, states that Jesus gave a linen cloth to the servant of the priest preceding his appearance to James. Some sources believe the linen cloth may have been the burial shroud, although they do not state if it had any images on it

Scientific perspective

The term sindonology (from the Greek σινδών—sindon, the word used in the Gospel of Mark[15:46] to describe the type of the burial cloth of Jesus) is used to refer to the formal study of the Shroud.

Secondo Pia's 1898 photographs of the shroud allowed the scientific community to begin to study it. A variety of scientific theories regarding the shroud have since been proposed, based on disciplines ranging from chemistry to biology and medical forensics to optical image analysis. The scientific approaches to the study of the Shroud fall into three groups: material analysis (both chemical and historical), biology and medical forensics and image analysis.

Early studies

The initial steps towards the scientific study of the shroud were taken soon after the first set of black and white photographs became available early in the 20th century. In 1902 Yves Delage, a French professor of comparative anatomy published the first study on the subject. Delage declared the image anatomically flawless and argued that the features of rigor mortis, wounds, and blood flows were evidence that the image was formed by direct or indirect contact with a corpse. William Meacham mentions several other medical studies between 1936 and 1981 that agree with Delage. However, these were all indirect studies without access to the shroud itself.

The first direct examination of the shroud by a scientific team was undertaken in 1969–1973 in order to advise on preservation of the shroud and determine specific testing methods. This led to the appointment of an 11-member Turin Commission to advise on the preservation of the relic and on specific testing. Five of the commission members were scientists, and preliminary studies of samples of the fabric were conducted in 1973.

In 1976 physicist John P. Jackson, thermodynamicist Eric Jumper and photographer William Mottern used image analysis technologies developed in aerospace science for analyzing the images of the Shroud. In 1977 these three scientists and over thirty others formed the Shroud of Turin Research Project. In 1978 this group, often called STURP, was given direct access to the Shroud.

Material chemical analysis

(Radiocarbon dating)

After years of discussion, the Holy See permitted radiocarbon dating on portions of a swatch taken from a corner of the shroud. Independent tests in 1988 at the University of Oxford, the University of Arizona, and the Swiss Federal Institute of Technology concluded with 95% confidence that the shroud material dated to 1260–1390 AD. This 13th to 14th century dating is much too recent for the shroud to have been associated with Jesus of Nazareth. The dating does on the other hand match the first appearance of the shroud in church history. This dating is also slightly more recent than that estimated by art historian W.S.A. Dale, who postulated on artistic grounds that the shroud is an 11th-century icon made for use in worship services.

Phase contrast microscopic view of image-bearing fiber from the Shroud of Turin. The carbohydrate layer is visible along top edge. The lower-right edge shows that coating is missing. The coating can be scraped off or removed with adhesive or diimide.

The repair hypothesis

Although the quality of the radiocarbon testing itself is unquestioned, criticisms have been raised regarding the choice of the sample taken for testing, with suggestions that the sample may represent a medieval "invisible" repair fragment rather than the image-bearing cloth.

The official report of the dating process, written by the people who performed the sampling, states that the sample "came from a single site on the main body of the shroud away from any patches or charred areas."[69] In 2008 former STURP member John Jackson rejected the possibility that the C14 sample may have been conducted on a medieval repair fragment, on the basis that the radiographs and transmitted light images taken by STURP in 1978 clearly show that the natural colour bandings present throughout the linen of the shroud propagate in an uninterrupted fashion through the region that would later provide the sample for radiocarbon dating. Jackson stated that this could not have been possible if the sampled area was a later addition.

Mechthild Flury-Lemberg is an expert in the restoration of textiles, who headed the restoration and conservation of the Turin Shroud in 2002. She has written that it's possible to repair a coarsely woven fabric in such a way as to be invisible, if the damage was not too severe and the original warp threads are still present, but that it is never possible to repair a fine fabric in a way which would be truly invisible, as the repair will always be "unequivocally visible on the reverse of the fabric." She criticized the theory that the C14 tests were done on an invisible patch as "wishful thinking". She states that Gabriel Vial, a textile expert who was present when the sample was taken, confirmed repeatedly that the sample was taken from the original cloth, and that "neither on the front nor on the back of the whole cloth is the slightest hint of a mending operation, a patch or some kind of reinforcing darning, to be found."

In December 2010 Professor Timothy Jull, a member of the original 1988 radiocarbon-dating team and editor of the peer-reviewed journal Radiocarbon, coauthored an article with a textile expert in that journal. They examined a portion of the radiocarbon sample left over from the section used by the University of Arizona in 1988 for the carbon dating exercise, and found no evidence of a repair, nor of any dyes or other treatments. They concluded that the radiocarbon dating had been performed on a sample of the original shroud material.

Since the C14 dating at least four articles have been published in scholarly sources contending that the samples used for the dating test may not have been representative of the whole shroud. These included a 2005 article by Raymond Rogers, who conducted chemical analysis for the Shroud of Turin Research Project and who was involved in work with the Shroud since the STURP project began in 1978. Rogers stated that after further study he was convinced that: "The worst possible sample for carbon dating was taken." However such findings are disputed by Professor Christopher Ramsey of the Oxford Radiocarbon Accelerator Unit, who stated in 2011 that "There are various hypotheses as to why the dates might not be correct, but none of them stack up."

In 2010, professors of statistics Marco Riani and Anthony C. Atkinson wrote in a scientific paper that the statistical analysis of the raw dates obtained from the three laboratories for the radiocarbon test suggests the presence of contamination in some of the samples. They conclude that: "The effect is not large over the sampled region ... our estimate of the change is about two centuries." The scientists who conducted the carbon-dating tests had originally attributed this minor variation to the fact that linen (flax) has a short growth period and is thus inherently variable compared to wood, as well as to the fact that every sample was cleaned with a different treatment method.[69]

Professor H E Gove, of the Nuclear Structure Research Laboratory at the University of Rochester, New York, stated re the repair hypothesis that "Even modern so-called invisible weaving can readily be detected under a microscope, so this possibility seems unlikely. It seems very convincing that what was measured in the laboratories was genuine cloth from the shroud after it had been subjected to rigorous cleaning procedures. Probably no sample for carbon dating has ever been subjected to such scrupulously careful examination and treatment, nor perhaps ever will again.

The contamination hypothesis

Bacteria and associated residue (bacteria by-products and dead bacteria) carry additional carbon-14 that would skew the radiocarbon date toward the present. In 1993 Dr. Leoncio A. Garza-Valdes discovered the presence of polyhydroxyalkanoate (mcl-PHA)-producing bacteria Leobacillus rubrus on Shroud fabric and stated that while studying thin sections from the Shroud fibers he found that "more than 60% of the fibers' area is bioplastic".

However Professor Harry Gove, director of Rochester's laboratory (one of the laboratories not selected to conduct the testing), STURP scientist Dr John Jackson and radiocarbon expert Rodger Sparks have all calculated that about two thirds of the sample would need to consist of modern material to swing the result away from a 1st Century date to a Medieval date. Gove and Jackson specifically noted that the samples had been carefully cleaned with different techniques before testing,[81][82][69] and Gove actually inspected the Arizona sample material before it was cleaned, and determined that no such gross amount of contamination was present even before the cleaning commenced. Fibers from the shroud were examined at the National Science Foundation Mass Spectrometry Center of Excellence at the University of Nebraska, where pyrolysis-mass-spectrometry examination failed to detect any form of bioplastic polymer on fibers from either non-image or image areas of the shroud. Additionally, laser-microprobe Raman analysis at Instruments SA, Inc. in Metuchen, New Jersey, also failed to detect any bioplastic polymer on shroud fibers.

Others have suggested that the silver of the molten reliquiary and the water used to douse the flames may have catalysed the airborne carbon into the cloth. Dmitri Kouznetsov, an archaeological biologist and chemist, claimed in 1994 to have experimentally reproduced this purported enrichment of the cloth in ancient weaves, and published numerous articles on the subject. Kouznetsov's results could not be replicated, and no other experiments has been able to validate this theory. Professor Gian Marco Rinaldi and others proved that Kouznetsov never performed the experiments described in his papers.

It has also been proposed that a reaction with carbon monoxide could add additional "fresh" C14 to the sample. However carbon monoxide does not undergo significant reactions with linen which could result in an incorporation of a significant number of CO molecules into the cellulose structure.

Tests for pigments

In 1970s a special eleven-member Turin Commission conducted several tests. Conventional and electron microscopic examination of the Shroud at that time revealed an absence of heterogeneous coloring material or pigment. In 1979, Walter McCrone, upon analyzing the samples he was given by STURP, concluded that the image is actually made up of billions of submicrometre pigment particles. The only fibrils that had been made available for testing of the stains were those that remained affixed to custom-designed adhesive tape applied to thirty-two different sections of the image.

Mark Anderson, who was working for McCrone, analyzed the Shroud samples.[101] In his book Ray Rogers states that Anderson, who was McCrone's Raman microscopy expert, observed that the samples acted as organic material when he subjected them to the laser, but McCrone refused to accept the observation for he wanted the conclusion that the image was painted with hematite. In his open letter to journalists Daniel R. Porter states that McCrone suppressed the results of Anderson.

John Heller and Alan Adler examined the same samples and agreed with McCrone's result that the cloth contains iron oxide. However, they concluded, the exceptional purity of the chemical and comparisons with other ancient textiles showed that, while retting flax absorbs iron selectively, the iron itself was not the source of the image on the shroud. Other microscopic analysis of the fibers seems to indicate that the image is strictly limited to the carbohydrate layer, with no additional layer of pigment visible

Material historical analysis

(Historical fabrics)

In 2000, fragments of a burial shroud from the 1st century were discovered in a tomb near Jerusalem, believed to have belonged to a Jewish high priest or member of the aristocracy. The shroud was composed of a simple two-way weave, unlike the complex herringbone twill of the Turin Shroud. Based on this discovery, the researchers stated that the Turin Shroud did not originate from Jesus-era Jerusalem. However, according to biblical scholar Diana Fulbright, the assumption made by Shimon Gibson and others is "over-reaching, without foundation and contradictory to abundant archeological evidence".

According to textile expert Mechthild Flury-Lemberg of Hamburg, a seam in the cloth corresponds to a fabric found at the fortress of Masada near the Dead Sea, which dated to the

1st century. The weaving pattern, 3:1 twill, is consistent with first-century Syrian design, according to the appraisal of Gilbert Raes of the Ghent Institute of Textile Technology in Belgium. Flury-Lemberg stated, "The linen cloth of the Shroud of Turin does not display any weaving or sewing techniques which would speak against its origin as a high-quality product of the textile workers of the first century."[111]

In 1999, Mark Guscin investigated the relationship between the shroud and the Sudarium of Oviedo, believed to be the cloth that covered the head of Jesus in the Gospel of John[20:6-7] when the empty tomb was discovered. The Sudarium is reported to have type AB blood stains. Guscin concluded that the two cloths covered the same head at two distinct, but close moments of time. Avinoam Danin (see below) concurred with this analysis, adding that the pollen grains in the Sudarium match those of the shroud. Skeptics criticize the polarized image overlay technique of Guscin and suggest that pollen from Jerusalem could have followed any number of paths to find its way to the sudarium.

In 2002, Aldo Guerreschi and Michele Salcito argued that many of these marks on the fabric of the shroud stem from a much earlier time because the symmetries correspond more to the folding that would have been necessary to store the cloth in a clay jar (like cloth samples at Qumran) than to that necessary to store it in the reliquary that housed it in 1532.

Above picture shows a Roman Loom from about the time of the repairs on the shroud.

Dirt Particles were also found to be present in the cloth. Joseph Kohlbeck from the Hercules

Aerospace Company in Utah and Richard Levi-Setti of the Enrico Fermi Institute examined some dirt particles from the Shroud surface. The dirt was found to be travertine aragonite limestone. Using a high-resolution microprobe, Levi-Setti and Kolbeck compared the spectra of samples taken from the Shroud with samples of limestone from ancient Jerusalem tombs. The chemical signatures of the Shroud samples and the tomb limestone were found identical except for minute fragments of cellulose linen fiber that could not be separated from the Shroud samples.

Biological and medical forensics

(Blood stains)

There are several reddish stains on the shroud suggesting blood, but it is uncertain whether these stains were produced at the same time as the image, or afterwards. McCrone (see painting hypothesis) identified these as containing iron oxide, theorizing that its presence was likely due to simple pigment materials used in medieval times. Other researchers, including Alan Adler, identified the reddish stains as blood and interpreted the iron oxide as a natural residue of hemoglobin.

Heller and Adler further studied the dark red stains and identified hemoglobin, as well as the presence of porphyrin, bilirubin, albumin, and protein.[118] Working independently, forensic pathologist Pier Luigi Baima Bollone concurred with Heller and Adler's findings and identified the blood as the AB blood group.[119] Subsequently, STURP sent flecks from the shroud to the laboratory devoted to the study of ancient blood at the State University of New York (SUNY), Binghamton. Dr. Andrew Merriwether at SUNY stated that it is almost certain that the flecks are blood, but that no definitive statements can be made about its nature or provenance, i.e., whether it is male or from the Near East. He also stated that no blood typing could be confirmed, as the DNA was badly fragmented.

Joe Nickell argues that results similar to Heller and Adler's could be obtained from tempera paint. Skeptics also cite other forensic blood tests whose results dispute the authenticity of the Shroud[113] that the blood could belong to a person handling the shroud, and that the apparent blood flows on the shroud are unrealistically neat.

Flowers and Pollen

In 1997 Avinoam Danin, a botanist at the Hebrew University of Jerusalem, reported that he had identified the type of Chrysanthemum coronarium, Cistus creticus and Zygophyllum whose pressed image on the shroud was first noticed by Alan Whanger in 1985 on the photographs of the shroud taken in 1931. He reported that the outlines of the flowering plants would point to March or April and the environs of Jerusalem. In a separate report in 1978 Danin and Uri Baruch reported on the pollen grains on the cloth samples, stating that they were appropriate to the spring in Israel. Max Frei, a Swiss police criminologist who initially obtained pollen from the shroud during the STURP investigation stated that of the 58 different types of pollens found, 45 were from the Jerusalem area, while 6 were from the eastern Middle East, with one pollen species growing exclusively in Constantinople, and two found in Edessa, Turkey. Mark Antonacci argues that the pollen evidence and flower images are inherently interwoven and strengthen each other.

Skeptics have argued that the flower images are too faint for Danin's determination to be definite, that an independent review of the pollen strands showed that one strand out of the 26 provided contained significantly more pollen than the others, perhaps pointing to deliberate contamination. Skeptics also argue that Max Frei had previously been duped in his examination of the Hitler Diaries and that he may have also been duped in this case, or may have introduced the pollens himself. J. Beaulieau has stated that Frei was a self-taught amateur palynologist, was not properly trained, and that his sample was too small.

In 2008 Avinoam Danin reported analysis based on the ultraviolet photographs of Miller and Pellicori[15][16] taken in 1978. Danin reported five new species of flower, which also bloom in March and April and stated that a comparison of the 1931 black and white photographs and the 1978 ultraviolet images indicate that the flower images are genuine and not the artifact of a specific method of photography.

Anatomical forensics

A number of studies on the anatomical consistency of the image on the shroud and the nature of the wounds on it have been performed, following the initial study by Yves Delage in 1902. While Delage declared the image anatomically flawless, others have presented arguments to support both authenticity and forgery.

In 1950 physician Pierre Barbet wrote a long study called A Doctor at Calvary which was later published as a book. Barbet stated that his experience as a battlefield surgeon during World War I led him to conclude that the image on the shroud was authentic, anatomically correct and consistent with crucifixion.

In 1997 physician and forensic pathologist Robert Bucklin constructed a scenario of how a systematic autopsy on the man of the shroud would have been conducted. He noted the series of traumatic injuries which extend from the shoulder areas to the lower portion of the back, which he considered consistent with whipping; and marks on the right shoulder blade which he concluded were signs of carrying a heavy object. Bucklin concluded that the image was of a real person, subject to crucifixion.

For over a decade, medical examiner Frederick Zugibe performed a number of studies using himself and volunteers suspended from a cross, and presented his conclusions in a book in 1998. Zugibe considered the shroud image and its proportions as authentic, but disagreed with Barbet and Bucklin on various details such as blood flow. Zugibe concluded that the image on the shroud is of the body of a man, but that the body had been washed.

In 2001, Pierluigi Baima Bollone, a professor of forensic medicine in Turin, stated that the forensic examination of the wounds and bloodstains on the Shroud indicate that the image was that of the dead body of a man who was whipped, wounded around the head by a pointed instrument and nailed at the extremities before dying.

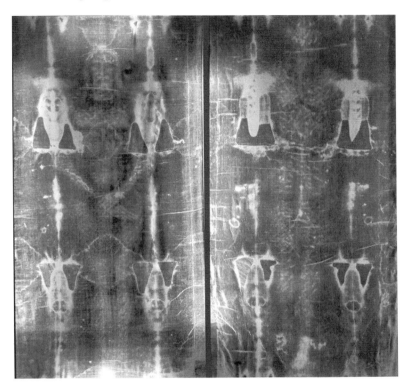

Above picture shows a divided view of the shroud so you can see both the front and back of the body standing next to one another.

The detail in the pictures is clear evidence of the crucifixion, death and burial of Jesus Christ.

It is also in my opinion absolute proof that he rose from the dead on the third day.

In 2010 Giulio Fanti, professor of mechanical measurements, wrote that "apart from the hands afterward placed on the pubic area, the front and back images are compatible with the Shroud being used to wrap the body of a man 175±2 cm (5 ft 9 in ± 1 in) tall, which, due to cadaveric rigidity, remained in the same position it would have assumed during crucifixion".

Artist Isabel Piczek stated in 1995 that while a general research opinion sees a flatly reclining body on the Shroud, the professional figurative artist can see substantial differences from a flatly reclining position. She stated that the professional arts cannot find discrepancies and distortions in the anatomy of the "Shroud Man".

Nickell, in 1983, and Gregory S. Paul in 2010, separately state that the proportions of the image are not realistic. Paul stated that the face and proportions of the shroud image are impossible, that the figure cannot represent that of an actual person and that the posture was inconsistent. They argued that the forehead on the shroud is too small; and that the arms are too long and of different lengths and that the distance from the eyebrows to the top of the head is non-representative. They concluded that the features can be explained if the shroud is a work of a Gothic artist.

Image and text analysis

(Image analysis)

Both digital image processing and analog techniques have been applied to the shroud images.

In 1976 Pete Schumacher, John Jackson and Eric Jumper analysed a photograph of the shroud image using a VP8 Image Analyzer, which was developed for NASA to create 3D images of the moon. They found that, unlike any photograph they had analyzed, the shroud image has the property of decoding into a 3-dimensional image, when the darker parts of the image are interpreted to be those features of the man that were closest to the shroud and the lighter areas of the image those features that were farthest. The researchers could not replicate the effect when they attempted to transfer similar images using techniques of block print, engravings, a hot statue, and bas-relief.

However optical physicist and former STURP member John Dee German has since noted that it is not difficult to make a photograph which has 3D qualities. If the object being photographed is lighted from the front, and a non-reflective "fog" of some sort exists between the camera and the object, then less light will reach and reflect back from the portions of the object that are farther from the lens, thus creating a contrast which is dependent on distance.

Shroud researcher Colin Berry has observed that the scorch marks and holes in the shroud also produced clear 3D images under the VP8 analysis. He deduced from this that the shroud image was produced by light scorching, and has produced 3D images from scorches using appropriate software.

NASA researchers Jackson, Jumper, and Stephenson report detecting the impressions of coins placed on both eyes after a digital study in 1978. They saw a two-lepton coin on the right eyelid dating from 29-30, and a one-lepton coin on the left eyebrow minted in 29. The existence of the coin images is rejected by most scientists.

In 2004, in an article in Journal of Optics A, Fanti and Maggiolo reported finding a faint second face on the backside of the cloth, after the 2002 restoration.

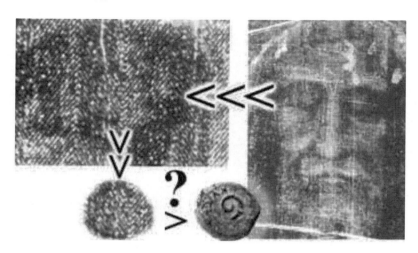

The front image of the Turin Shroud, 1.95 m long, is not directly compatible with the back image, 2.02 m long.

Text of death certificate

A late 19th-century photograph of the Chapel of the Shroud

In 1979 Greek and Latin letters were reported as written near the face. These were further studied by André Marion, professor at the École supérieure d'optique and his student Anne

Laure Courage, in 1997. Subsequently, after performing computerized analysis and microdensitometer studies, they reported finding additional inscriptions, among them INNECEM (a shortened form of Latin "in necem ibis"—"you will go to death"), NNAZAPE(N)NUS (Nazarene), IHSOY (Jesus) and IC (Iesus Chrestus). The uncertain letters IBE(R?) have been conjectured as "Tiberius". Linguist Mark Guscin disputed the reports of Marion and Courage. He stated that the inscriptions made little grammatical or historical sense and that they did not appear on the slides that Marion and Courage indicated.

In 2009, Barbara Frale, a paleographer in the Vatican Secret Archives, who had published two books on the Shroud of Turin reported further analysis of the text. In her books Frale had stated that the shroud had been kept by the Templars after 1204. In 2009 Frale stated that it is possible to read on the image the burial certificate of Jesus the Nazarene, or Jesus of Nazareth, imprinted in fragments of Greek, Hebrew and Latin writing.

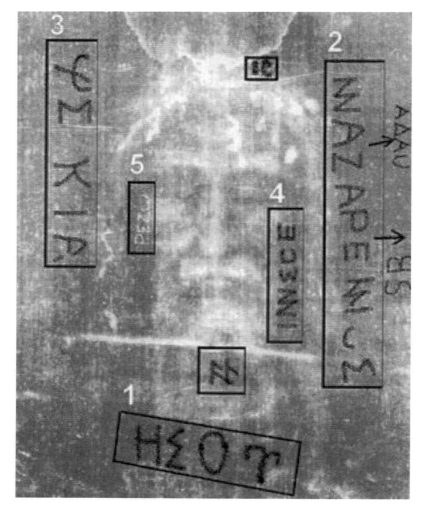

Frale stated the text on the Shroud reads: "In the year 16 of the reign of the Emperor Tiberius Jesus the Nazarene, taken down in the early evening after having been condemned to death by a Roman judge because he was found guilty by a Hebrew authority, is hereby sent for burial with the obligation of being consigned to his family only after one full year." Since Tiberius became emperor after the death of Octavian Augustus in AD 14, the 16th year of his reign would be within the span of the years AD 30 to 31. Frale's methodology has been criticized, partly based on the objection that the writings are too faint to see.[163][164][165] Dr Antonio Lombatti, an Italian historian, rejected the idea that the authorities would have bothered to tag the body of a crucified man. He stated that "It's all the result of imagination and computer software."

A more recent study by Lorusso et al. subjected two photographs of the shroud to detailed modern digital image processing, one of them being a reproduction of the photographic negative taken by Giuseppe Enrie in 1931. They did not find any signs, symbols or writing on either image, and noted that these signs may be linked to protuberances in the yarn, as well possibly as to the alteration and influence of the texture of the Enrie photographic negative during its development in 1931.

Hypotheses on image origin

Many hypotheses have been formulated and tested to explain the image on the Shroud. According to pro-authenticity authors Baldacchini and Fanti to date, "the body image of the Turin Shroud has not yet been explained by traditional science; so a great interest in a possible mechanism of image formation still exists", a conclusion also supported by Philip Ball.

Painting and pigmentation

(Painting)

The technique used for producing the image is, according to W. McCrone, already described in a book about medieval painting published in 1847 by Charles Lock Eastlake ("Methods and Materials of Painting of the Great Schools and Masters"). Eastlake describes in the chapter "Practice of Painting Generally During the XIVth Century" a special technique of painting on linen using tempera paint, which produces images with unusual transparent features—which McCrone compares to the image on the shroud.

Pro-authenticity journals have declared this hypothesis to be unsound, stating that X-ray fluorescence examination, as well as infrared thermography, did not point out any pigment.

It was also found that 25 different solvents, among them water, do not reduce or sponge out the image. The non-paint origin has been further examined by Fourier transform of the image: common paintings show a directionality that is absent from the Turin Shroud. However McCrone and others have confirmed the presence of pigments, of types commonly used in medieval paints, on the shroud.

Bishop D'Arcis's letter to Pope Clement VII, the earliest reference to the shroud, states that the forger who confessed to making it had done so by painting.

The Shroud Center of Colorado states that paint pigments came from painted copies that were overlaid by artists during the Middle Ages in order to validate them as accurate copies of the Shroud.

Acid pigmentation

In 2009, Luigi Garlaschelli, professor of organic chemistry at the University of Pavia, announced that he had made a full size reproduction of the Shroud of Turin using only medieval technologies. Garlaschelli placed a linen sheet over a volunteer and then rubbed it with an acidic pigment. The shroud was then aged in an oven before being washed to remove the pigment. He then added blood stains, scorches and water stains to replicate the original.[177] But according to Giulio Fanti, professor of mechanical and thermic measurements at the University of Padua, "the technique itself seems unable to produce an image having the most critical Turin Shroud image characteristics".

Medieval photography

According to the art historian Nicholas Allen the image on the shroud was formed by a photographic technique in the 13th century. Allen maintains that techniques already available before the 14th century—e.g., as described in the Book of Optics, which was at just that time translated from Arabic to Latin— were sufficient to produce primitive photographs, and that people familiar with these techniques would have been able to produce an image as found on the shroud. To demonstrate this, he successfully produced photographic images similar to the shroud using only techniques and materials available at the time the shroud was made. He described his results in his PhD thesis, in papers published in several science journals, and in a book. Silver bromide is believed by some to have been used for making the Shroud of Turin as it is widely used in photographic films.

Lynn Picknett has written a book proposing that Leonardo da Vinci had faked the Shroud. Picknett and Larissa Tracy appeared on a Channel 5 (UK) TV program that announced that the Shroud was the oldest known surviving photograph. The program theorized that da Vinci used a real corpse, obtained an old-looking piece of linen, treated it with photo-sensitive chemicals and then exposed it in an early form of camera obscura to create the image. However John Jackson, director of the Turin Shroud Centre of Colorado dismissed these hypotheses. Jackson et al. have argued that a double photographic exposure, needed in that case, should have considered the distances and in this case there would be areas of photographic superimposition with different lights and shades. The distances on Shroud instead correspond to the body position

The above picture shows the comparison of the shroud to a very early artist rendering of Christ. Showing the shroud may have well been his

guide for the painting. (dating it before the carbon dating results).

Dust-transfer technique

Scientists Emily Craig and Randall Bresee have attempted to recreate the likenesses of the shroud through the dust-transfer technique, which could have been done by medieval arts. They first did a carbon-dust drawing of a Jesus-like face (using collagen dust) on a newsprint made from wood pulp (which is similar to 13th and 14th-century paper). They next placed the drawing on a table and covered it with a piece of linen. They then pressed the linen against the newsprint by firmly rubbing with the flat side of a wooden spoon. By doing this they managed to create a reddish brown image with a lifelike positive likeness of a person, a three dimensional image and no sign of brush strokes. However, according to Fanti and Moroni, this does not reproduce many special features of the Shroud at microscopic level

Bas-relief

Another hypothesis suggests that the Shroud may have been formed using a bas-relief sculpture. Researcher Jacques di Costanzo, noting that the Shroud image seems to have a three-dimensional quality, suggested that perhaps the image was formed using an actual three-dimensional object, such as a sculpture. While wrapping a cloth around a life-sized statue would result in a distorted image, placing a cloth over a bas-relief would result in an image like the one seen on the shroud. To demonstrate the plausibility of his hypothesis, Costanzo constructed a bas-relief of a Jesus-like face and draped wet linen over the bas-relief. After the linen dried, he dabbed it with a mixture of ferric oxide and gelatine. The result was an image similar to that of the Shroud. The imprinted image turned out to be wash-resistant, impervious to temperatures of 250 °C (482 °F) and was undamaged by exposure to a range of harsh chemicals, including bisulphite which, without the help of the gelatine, would normally have degraded ferric oxide to the compound ferrous oxide.[191] Similar results have been obtained by Nickell.

Instead of painting, it has been suggested that the bas-relief could also be heated and used to scorch an image onto the cloth. However researcher Thibault Heimburger performed some experiments with the scorching of linen, and found that a scorch mark is only produced by direct contact with the hot object – thus producing an all-or-nothing discoloration with no graduation of color as is found in the shroud.

According to Fanti and Moroni, after comparing the histograms of 256 different grey levels, it was found that the image obtained with a bas-relief has grey values included between 60 and 256 levels, but it is much contrasted with wide areas of white saturation (levels included between 245 and 256) and lacks of intermediate grey levels (levels included between 160 and 200). The face image on the Shroud instead has grey tonalities that vary in the same values field (between 60 and 256), but the white saturation is much less marked and the histogram is practically flat in correspondence of the intermediate grey levels (levels included between 160 and 200).

Maillard reaction

The Maillard reaction is a form of non-enzymatic browning involving an amino acid and a reducing sugar. The cellulose fibers of the shroud are coated with a thin carbohydrate layer of starch fractions, various sugars, and other impurities. In a paper entitled "The Shroud of Turin: an amino-carbonyl reaction may explain the image formation," Raymond Rogers and Anna Arnoldi propose that amines from a recently deceased human body may have undergone Maillard reactions with this carbohydrate layer within a reasonable period of time, before liquid decomposition products stained or damaged the cloth. The gases produced by a dead body are extremely reactive chemically and within a few hours, in an environment such as a tomb, a body starts to produce heavier amines in its tissues such as putrescine and cadaverine. However the potential source for amines required for the reaction is a decomposing body, and no signs of decomposition have been found on the Shroud.[196] Rogers also notes that their tests revealed that there were no proteins or bodily fluids on the image areas. Also, the image resolution and the uniform coloration of the linen resolution seem to be incompatible with a mechanism involving diffusion.

Alan A. Mills argued that the image was formed by the chemical reaction auto-oxidation. He noted that the image corresponds to what would have been produced by a volatile chemical if the intensity of the color change were inversely proportional to the distance from the body of a loosely draped cloth.

The Garden Tomb

The Garden Tomb located in Jerusalem, outside the city walls and close to the Damascus Gate, is a rock-cut tomb which was unearthed in 1867 and has subsequently been considered by some Christians to be the site of the burial and resurrection of Jesus. The Garden Tomb is adjacent to a rocky escarpment which since the mid-nineteenth century has been proposed by some scholars to be Golgotha (it is also known as Skull Hill[1] and Gordon's Calvary[2]). In contradistinction to this modern identification the traditional site where the death and resurrection of Christ are believed to have occurred has been the Church of the Holy Sepulchre at least since the fourth century.

Since 1894 the Garden Tomb and its surrounding gardens have been maintained as a place of Christian worship and reflection

Corona discharge

During restoration in 2002, the back of the cloth was photographed and scanned for the first time. An article on this subject by Giulio Fanti and others envisages the electrostatic corona discharge as the probable mechanism to produce the images of the body in the Shroud. Congruent with that mechanism, they also describe an image on the reverse side of the fabric, much fainter than that on the front view of the body, consisting primarily of the face and perhaps hands. As with the front picture, it is entirely superficial, with coloration limited to the carbohydrate layer. The images correspond to, and are in registration with, those on the other side of the cloth. No image is detectable in the reverse side of the dorsal view of the body.

In December 2011 Giulio Fanti, a scientist at the University of Padua, published a critical compendium of the major hypotheses regarding the formation of the body image on the shroud. Fanti stated that "none of them can completely explain the mysterious image". Fanti then considered corona discharge as the most probable hypothesis regarding the formation of the body image. He stated that it would be impossible to reproduce all the characteristics of the image in a laboratory because the energy source required would be too high. Fanti has restated the radiation theories in a 2013 book.

Raymond Rogers, who conducted chemical analysis for the Shroud of Turin Research Project, stated that corona discharges and/or plasmas could have made no contribution to image formation because: "It is clear that a corona discharge (plasma) in air will cause easily observable changes in a linen sample. No such effects can be observed in image fibers from the Shroud of Turin."

Ultraviolet radiation

In December 2011 scientists at Italy's National Agency for New Technologies, Energy and Sustainable Development ENEA deduced from the STURP results that the color of the Shroud image is the result of an accelerated aging process of the linen, similar to the yellowing of the paper of ancient books. They demonstrated that the photochemical reactions caused by exposing linen to ultraviolet light could reproduce the main characteristics of the Shroud image, such as the shallowness of the coloration and the gradient of the color, which are not reproducible by other means. When subsequently illuminated with a UV lamp, the irradiated linen fabrics behaved like the linen of the Shroud. They also determined that UV radiation changes the crystalline structure of cellulose in a similar manner as aging and long-duration background radiation.

Professor Paolo Di Lazzaro, the lead researcher, indicated in an e-mail interview that '....it appears unlikely a forger may have done this image with technologies available in the

Middle Ages or earlier', but their study does not mean the Shroud image was created by the flash of a miraculous resurrection, contrary to how the story was presented in the media, especially on the Web. Prominent skeptic Joe Nickell, however, is not impressed with the news. He indicates the latest findings are nothing new despite being 'dressed up in high-tech tests' and doesn't prove much of anything.

Recent developments

A team of graphic artists tried to recreate the real face of the man depicted on the cloth in a special two-hour documentary on the History Channel broadcast for the first time in March 2010. The image was made by taking the image of the Turin Shroud and transforming it onto a 3D form to compose and inspire a CGI image of a detailed face.

In November 2011, F. Curciarello et al. published a paper that analyzed the abrupt changes in the yellowed fibril density values on the Shroud image. They concluded that the rapid changes in the body image intensity are not anomalies in the manufacturing process of the linen but that they can be explained with the presence of aromas or burial ointments. However, their work leaves the existence of an energy source for the image an open question.

In his 2012 book The Sign, art historian Thomas de Wesselow has written that he has come to view the shroud as genuine. In the book he argues that the image on the Shroud—which he sees as most likely the result of a Maillard reaction—caused the disciples to believe that Jesus had resurrected, but he does not support the historicity of the resurrection itself.

In 2013, Giulio Fanti and Saverio Gaeta, a former Vatican journalist, published a book in which they dated the shroud to between 280 BC and 220 AD. Fanti and his colleagues conducted a variety of mechanical and chemical tests on fibers from the shroud to obtain their date. In 2013 Fanti published a paper explaining that he had invented and calibrated these tests himself, and that they derived an origin for the tested fibers of 400AD, but with an error margin of 400 years due to the unknown influences of temperature and humidity on the samples during their lives. Cesare Nosiglia, Archbishop of Turin and Custodian of the Holy Shroud, responded that "as it is not possible to be certain that the analyzed material was taken from the fabric of the Shroud, the Holy See and the Papal Custodian declare that no serious value can be recognized to the results of such experiments."

On Holy Saturday (30 March) 2013, images of the shroud were streamed on various websites as well as on television for the first time in 40 years. Roberto Gottardo of the diocese of Turin stated that for the first time ever they had released high definition images of the shroud that can be used on tablet computers and can be magnified to show details not visible to the naked eye. As this rare exposition took place, Pope Francis issued a carefully worded statement which urged the faithful to contemplate the shroud with awe, but "stopped firmly short of asserting its authenticity", as his predecessors had done before him. The statement generated considerable comment.

In 2013, new peer-reviewed articles were published in favor of the hypothesis that the Turin shroud is the burial cloth of Jesus of Nazareth. One followed a "Minimal Facts approach" to determine which hypothesis relating to the image formation process "is the most likely". Another analysed the wounds seemingly evident on the image in the shroud and compared them to the wounds which the gospels state were inflicted on Jesus. Another regression analysis by Riani et al concluded that the validity of the 1988 radiocarbon dating test is questionable.

A team of researchers from the Politecnico di Torino, led by Professor Alberto Carpinteri, believe that if a magnitude 8.2 earthquake occurred in Jerusalem in 33 AD, it may have released sufficient radiation to have increased the level of carbon-14 isotopes in the shroud, which could skew carbon dating results, making the shroud appear younger. This hypothesis has been questioned by other scientists, including a radiocarbon-dating expert. The underlying science is widely disputed, and funding for the underlying research has been withdrawn by the Italian government after protests and pressure from more than 1000 Italian and international scientists. Dr REM Hedges, of the Radiocarbon Accelerator Unit of the University of Oxford, states that "the likelihood that [neutron irradiation] influenced the date in the way proposed is in my view so exceedingly remote that it beggars scientific credulity."

Sudarium of Oviedo

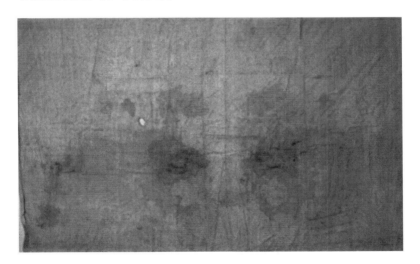

The Sudarium of Oviedo, or Shroud of Oviedo, is a bloodstained piece of cloth measuring c. 84 x 53 cm (33 x 21 inches) kept in the Cámara Santa of the Cathedral of San Salvador, Oviedo, Spain.[citation needed] The Sudarium (Latin for sweat cloth) is claimed by some to be the cloth wrapped around the head of Jesus Christ after he died, as mentioned in the Gospel of John (20:6-7). The small chapel housing it was built specifically for the cloth by King Alfonso II of Asturias in AD 840; the Arca Santa is an elaborate reliquary chest with a Romanesque metal frontal for the storage of the Sudarium and other relics. The Sudarium is displayed to the public three times a year: Good Friday, the Feast of the Triumph of the Cross on 14 September, and its octave on 21 September.

Background and history

The Sudarium is severely soiled and crumpled, with dark flecks that are symmetrically arranged but form no image, unlike the markings on the Shroud of Turin. Such an object is not mentioned in accounts of the actual burial of Jesus Christ, but is mentioned as having been present in the empty tomb later (John 20:7).

According to believers in the authenticity of the relic, the Sudarium and the Shroud took different routes. There is no reference of the

Sudarium for the first several hundred years after the Crucifixion of Jesus, until its mention in 570 in an account by Antoninus of Piacenza, who writes that the Sudarium is being cared for in a cave near the monastery of Saint Mark, in the vicinity of Jerusalem.

The Sudarium is presumed to have been taken from Palestine in 614, after the invasion of the Byzantine provinces by the Sassanid Persian King Khosrau II, was carried through northern Africa in 616 and arrived in Spain shortly thereafter.

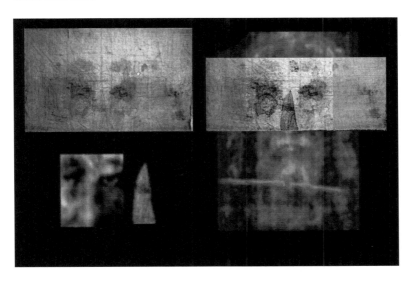

The cloth has been dated to around 700CE by the radio carbon method. This suggests a considerably earlier date than for most estimates for the Shroud of Turin, the previous three radiocarbon tests for which suggest a date between 1260AD and 1390AD,. Conversely, this date is younger than that suggested by the most recent analysis of the Shroud, which dates it to between 300BC and 400AD

Using infrared and ultraviolet photography and electron microscopy, research by the private Centro Español de Sindonología, (Spanish Centre for Sindonology) purported to show that that the Sudarium of Oviedo could have touched the same face as the Shroud of Turin, but at different stages after the death of the person. The researchers theorize that the Oviedo Cloth covered the face from the moment of death until replaced by the Turin Shroud. The researchers cite purported bloodstains on both cloths, identifying them as belonging to the same type, AB. No DNA testing, however, has been carried out on blood samples from either cloth. Pollen samples from both cloths share members of certain species – one example is the thorn bush Gundelia tournefortii, which is indigenous to the Mideast.

The fit between the bloodstains on the Sudarium and the Shroud is too close and complex to have been mere coincidence. Yet for this to have been the work of a forger, he would have had to have access to the Shroud of Turin. But as Freeman himself admits, the Sudarium was "in Spain ... in 1030," that is, 230 years before 1260 which is the earliest radiocarbon date of the Shroud!

The next section of this book is about the historical and biblical Jesus Christ, Our Lord and savior.

It has been taken from ancient writings, the gospels of the New Testament and historic facts.

JESUS CHRIST

Jesus (/ˈdʒiːzəs/; Greek: Ἰησοῦς Iesous; 7–2 BC to 30–33 AD), also referred to as Jesus of Nazareth, is the central figure of Christianity (the world's largest religion), whom the teachings of most Christian denominations hold to be the Son of God. Christianity regards Jesus as the awaited Messiah of the Old Testament and refers to him as Jesus Christ, a name that is also used in non-Christian contexts.

Virtually all modern scholars of antiquity agree that Jesus existed historically, although the quest for the historical Jesus has produced little agreement on the historical reliability of the Gospels and how closely the biblical Jesus reflects the historical Jesus. Most scholars agree that Jesus was a Jewish rabbi from Galilee who preached his message orally, was baptized by John the Baptist, and was crucified in Jerusalem on the orders of the Roman prefect, Pontius Pilate. Scholars have constructed various portraits of the historical Jesus, which often depict him as having one or more of the following roles: the leader of an apocalyptic movement, Messiah, a charismatic healer, a sage and philosopher, or an egalitarian social reformer. Scholars have correlated the New Testament accounts with non-Christian historical records to arrive at an estimated chronology of Jesus' life. The most widely used calendar era in the world, in which the current year is 2014 (abbreviated as "AD", alternatively referred to as "CE"), counts from a medieval estimate of the birth year of Jesus.

Christians believe that Jesus has a "unique significance" in the world. Christian doctrines include the beliefs that Jesus was conceived by the Holy Spirit, was born of a virgin, performed miracles, founded the Church, died by crucifixion as a sacrifice to achieve atonement, rose from the dead, and ascended into heaven, whence he will return. The great majority of Christians worship Jesus as the incarnation of God the Son, the second of three persons of a Divine Trinity. A few Christian groups reject Trinitarianism, wholly or partly, as non-scriptural.

In Islam, Jesus (commonly transliterated as Isa) is considered one of God's important prophets and the Messiah. To Muslims, Jesus is a bringer of scripture and the child of a virgin birth, but neither divine nor the victim of crucifixion. Judaism rejects the belief that Jesus was the awaited Messiah, arguing that he did not fulfill the Messianic prophecies in the Tanakh.

Etymology of names

Further information: Jesus (name), Holy Name of Jesus, Name of God in Christianity, and Yeshua (name)

Since early Christianity, Christians have commonly referred to Jesus as "Jesus Christ". The word Christ is derived from the Greek Χριστός (Christos), which is a translation of the Hebrew מָשִׁיחַ (Masiah), meaning the "anointed" and usually transliterated into English as "Messiah".

Christians designate Jesus as Christ because they believe he is the awaited Messiah prophesied in the Hebrew Bible (Old Testament). In postbiblical usage, Christ became viewed as a name—one part of "Jesus Christ"—but originally it was a title. The term "Christian" (meaning "one who owes allegiance to the person Christ" or simply "follower of Christ") has been in use since the first century

A typical Jew in Jesus' time had only one name, sometimes supplemented with the father's name or the individual's hometown.[26] Thus, in the New Testament, Jesus is referred to as

"Jesus of Nazareth"[f] (Matthew 26:71), "Joseph's son" (Luke 4:22), and "Jesus son of Joseph from Nazareth" (John 1:45). However, in Mark 6:3, rather than being called the son of Joseph, he is referred to as "the son of Mary and brother of James and Joses and Judas and Simon". The name Jesus, as found in several modern languages, is derived from the Latin Iesus, a transliteration of the Greek Ἰησοῦς (Iesous). The Greek form is a rendition of the Aramaic ישוע (Yeshua), which is derived from the Hebrew יהושע (Yehoshua). The name Yeshua appears to have been in use in Judea at the time of the birth of Jesus. The first-century works of historian Flavius Josephus (who wrote in Koine Greek, the same language as that of the New Testament) refer to at least twenty different people with the name Jesus (i.e. Ἰησοῦς). The etymology of Jesus' name in the context of the New Testament is generally given as "Yahweh is salvation".

The Birth of Jesus

Luke 2:1-20

New International Version (NIV)

2 In those days Caesar Augustus issued a decree that a census should be taken of the entire Roman world. 2 (This was the first census that took place while[a] Quirinius was governor of Syria.) 3 And everyone went to their own town to register.

4 So Joseph also went up from the town of Nazareth in Galilee to Judea, to Bethlehem the town of David, because he belonged to the house and line of David. 5 He went there to register with Mary, who was pledged to be married to him and was expecting a child. 6 While they were there, the time came for the baby to be born, 7 and she gave birth to her firstborn, a son. She wrapped him in cloths and placed him in a manger, because there was no guest room available for them.

8 And there were shepherds living out in the fields nearby, keeping watch over their flocks at night. 9 An angel of the Lord appeared to them, and the glory of the Lord shone around them, and they were terrified. 10 But the angel said to

them, "Do not be afraid. I bring you good news that will cause great joy for all the people. 11 Today in the town of David a Savior has been born to you; he is the Messiah, the Lord. 12 This will be a sign to you: You will find a baby wrapped in cloths and lying in a manger."

13 Suddenly a great company of the heavenly host appeared with the angel, praising God and saying,

14 "Glory to God in the highest heaven,

   and on earth peace to those on whom his favor rests."

15 When the angels had left them and gone into heaven, the shepherds said to one another, "Let's go to Bethlehem and see this thing that has happened, which the Lord has told us about."

16 So they hurried off and found Mary and Joseph, and the baby, who was lying in the

manger. 17 When they had seen him, they spread the word concerning what had been told them about this child, 18 and all who heard it were amazed at what the shepherds said to them. 19 But Mary treasured up all these things and pondered them in her heart. 20 The shepherds returned, glorifying and praising God for all the things they had heard and seen, which were just as they had been told.

Jesus Christ was born circa 6 B.C. in Bethlehem. Little is known about his early life, but as a young man, he founded Christianity, one of the world's most influential religions. His life is recorded in the New Testament, more a theological document than a biography. According to Christians, Jesus is considered the incarnation of God and his teachings an example for living a more spiritual life. Christians believe he died for the sins of all people and rose from the dead.

Background and Early Life

Most of Jesus's life is told through the four Gospels of the New Testament Bible, known as the Canonical gospels, written by Matthew, Mark, Luke and John. These are not biographies in the modern sense but accounts with allegorical intent. They are written to engender faith in Jesus as the Messiah and the incarnation of God, who came to teach, suffer and die for people's sins.

Jesus was born circa 6 B.C. in Bethlehem. His mother, Mary, was a virgin who was betrothed to Joseph, a carpenter. Christians believe Jesus was born through Immaculate Conception. His lineage can be traced back to the house of David. According to the Gospel of Matthew (2:1), Jesus was born during the reign of Herod the Great, who upon hearing of his birth felt threatened and tried to kill Jesus by ordering all of Bethlehem's male children under age two to be killed. But Joseph was warned by an angel and took Mary and the child to Egypt until Herod's death, where upon he brought the family back and settled in the town of Nazareth, in Galilee.

There is very little written about Jesus's early life. The Gospel of Luke (2:41-52) recounts that a 12-year-old Jesus had accompanied his parents on a pilgrimage to Jerusalem and became separated. He was found several days later in a temple, discussing affairs with some of Jerusalem's elders. Throughout the New Testament, there are trace references of Jesus working as a carpenter while a young adult. It is believed that he began his ministry at age 30 when he was baptized by John the Baptist, who upon seeing Jesus, declared him the Son of God.

After baptism, Jesus went into the Judean desert to fast and meditate for 40 days and nights. The Temptation of Christ is chronicled in the Gospels of Matthew, Mark and Luke (known as the Synoptic Gospels). The Devil appeared and tempted Jesus three times, once to turn stone to bread, once to cast himself off a mountain where angels would save him, and once to offer him all the kingdoms of the world. All three times, Jesus rejected the Devil's temptation and sent him off.

Jesus's Ministry

Jesus returned to Galilee and made trips to neighboring villages. During this time, several people became his disciples. One of these was Mary Magdalene, who is first mentioned the Gospel of Luke (16:9) and later in all four gospels at the crucifixion. Though not mentioned in the context of the "12 disciples," she is considered to have been involved in Jesus's ministry from the beginning to his death and after.

According to the gospels of Mark and John, Jesus appeared to Magdalene first after his resurrection.

According to the Gospel of John (2:1-11), as Jesus was beginning his ministry, he and his disciples traveled with his mother, Mary, to a wedding at Cana in Galilee. The wedding host had run out of wine and Jesus's mother came to him for help. At first, Jesus refused to intervene, but then he relented and asked a servant to bring him large jars filled with water.

He turned the water into a wine of higher quality than any served during the wedding. John's gospel depicts the event as the first sign of Jesus's glory and his disciples' belief in him.

After the wedding, Jesus, his mother Mary and his disciples traveled to Jerusalem for Passover. At the temple, they saw moneychangers and merchants selling wares. In a rare display of anger, Jesus overturned the tables and, with a whip made of cords, drove them out, declaring that his Father's house is not a house for merchants.

The Synoptic Gospels chronicle Jesus as he traveled through Judea and Galilee, using parables and miracles to explain how the prophecies were being fulfilled and that the kingdom of God was near. As word spread of Jesus's teaching and healing the sick and diseased, more people began to follow him. At one point, Jesus came to a level area and was joined by a great number of people. There, at the Sermon on the Mount, he presented several discourses, known as the Beatitudes, which encapsulate many of the spiritual teachings of love, humility and compassion.

As Jesus continued preaching about the kingdom of God, the crowds grew larger and began to proclaim him as the son of David and as the Messiah. The Pharisees heard of this and publicly challenged Jesus, accusing him of having the power of Satan. He defended his actions with a parable, then questioned their logic and told them such thinking denied the power of God, which only further hardened their resolve to work against him.

Near the city of Caesarea Philippi, Jesus talked with his disciples. According to the gospels of Matthew (16:13), Mark (8:27) and Luke (9:18), he asked, "Who do you say that I am?" The question confused them, and only Peter responded, saying, "You are the Christ, the Son of the living God." Jesus blessed Peter, accepting the titles of "Christ" and the "Son of God," and declared the proclamation was a divine revelation from God. Jesus then proclaimed Peter to be the leader of the church. Jesus then warned his disciples of the Pharisees' conspiracy against him and of his fate to suffer and be killed, only to rise from the dead on the third day.

Less than a week later, Jesus took three of his disciples to a high mountain where they could pray alone. According to the Synoptic Gospels, Jesus's face began shining like the sun and his entire body glowed with a white light. Then, the prophets Elijah and Moses appeared, and Jesus talked to them. A bright cloud emerged around them, and a voice said, "This is my beloved Son, with whom I am well pleased; listen to him." This event, known as the Transfiguration, is a pivotal moment in Christian theology.

It supports the identity of Jesus as the Christ, the Son of the living God.

Jesus arrived in Jerusalem, the week before the holiday of Passover, riding on a donkey. Great numbers of people took palm branches and greeted him at the city's entry. They praised him as the Son of David and as the Son of God. The priests and Pharisees, fearful of the growing public adulation, felt he must be stopped.

All four Gospels describe Jesus's final week in Jerusalem. During this time, Jesus raised Lazarus from the dead, confronted moneychangers and merchants in the temple, and debated with the high priests who questioned Jesus's authority. He told his disciples about the coming days and that Jerusalem's temple would be destroyed. Meanwhile, the chief priests and elders met with high priest Caiaphas, and set plans in motion to arrest Jesus. One of the disciples, Judas, met with the chief priests and told them how he would deliver Jesus to them. They agreed to pay him 30 pieces of silver.

The Last Supper

Jesus and his 12 disciples met for the Passover meal, and he gave them his final words of faith. He also foretold of his betrayal by one of the disciples and privately let Judas know it was he. Jesus told Peter that before a rooster crowed the next morning, he would have denied knowing Jesus three times. At the end of the meal, Jesus instituted the Eucharist, which in the Christian religion, signifies the covenant between God and humans.

After the Last Supper, Jesus and his disciples went to the Garden of Gethsemane to pray. Jesus asked God if this cup (his suffering and death) might pass by him. He implored a group of his disciples to pray with him, but they kept falling asleep. Then the time had come. Soldiers and officials appeared, and Judas was with them. He gave Jesus a kiss on the cheek to identify him and the soldiers arrested Jesus. One disciple tried to resist the arrest, brandished his sword and cut the ear off one of the soldiers. But Jesus admonished him and healed the soldier's wound.

After his arrest, many of the disciples went into hiding. Jesus was taken to the high priest and interrogated. He was hit and spat upon for not responding. Meanwhile, Peter had followed Jesus to the high priests' court. As he hid in the shadows, three house servants asked if he was one of Jesus' disciples and each time he denied it. After each denial, a rooster crowed. Then Jesus was led out of the house and looked directly at Peter. Peter remembered how Jesus had told him he would deny him and he wept bitterly. Judas, who was watching from a distance, became distraught by his betrayal of Jesus and attempted to return the 30 pieces of silver. The priests told him his guilt was his own. He threw the coins into the temple and later hanged himself.

The Crucifixion

The next day, Jesus was taken to the high court where he was mocked, beaten and condemned for claiming to be the Son of God. He was brought before Pontius Pilate, the Roman governor of Judea. The priests accused Jesus of claiming to be the king of the Jews and asked that he be condemned to death.

At first Pilate tried to pass Jesus off to King Herod, but he was brought back, and Pilate told the Jewish priests he could find no fault with Jesus. The priests reminded him that anyone who claimed to be a king speaks against Caesar. Pilate publicly washed his hands of responsibility, yet ordered the crucifixion in response to the demands of the crowd. The Roman soldiers whipped and beat Jesus, placed a crown of thorns on his head and then led him off to Mount Calvary.

Jesus was crucified with two thieves, one at his left and the other at his right. Above his head was the charge against him, "King of the Jews." At his feet were his mother, Mary, and Mary Magdalene.

The Gospels describe various events that occurred during the last three hours of his life, including the taunting by the soldiers and the crowd, Jesus's agony and outbursts, and his final words. While Jesus was on the cross, the sky darkened, and immediately upon his death, an earthquake erupted, tearing the temple's curtain from top to bottom. A soldier confirmed his death by sticking a spear into his side, which produced only water. He was taken down from the cross and buried in a nearby tomb.

Risen from the Dead

Three days after his death, Jesus's tomb was found empty. He had risen from the dead and appeared first to Mary Magdalene and then to his mother Mary. They both informed the disciples, who were in hiding, and later, Jesus appeared to them and told them not to be afraid. During this brief time, he beseeched his disciples to go into the world and preach the gospel to all humanity. After 40 days, Jesus led his disciples to Mount Olivet, east of Jerusalem. Jesus spoke his final words to them, saying that they would receive the power of the Holy Spirit, before he was taken upward on a cloud and ascended into heaven.

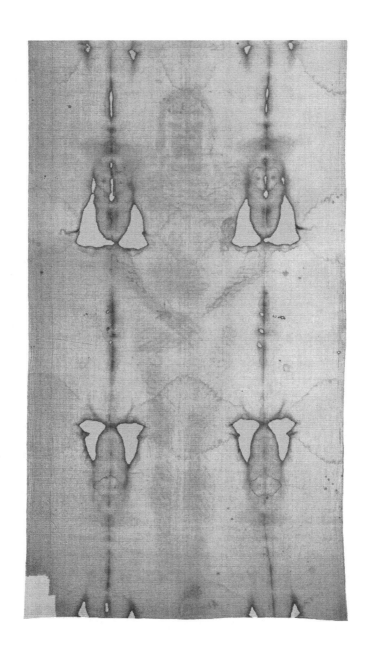

Made in the USA
San Bernardino, CA
07 May 2014